To all who still find it's good to talk

Introduction

When you are camping out, backpacking, or doing other outdoor adventures with others, there will be downtimes, pauses in the action. Being outdoors with others is often much more of a direct communicative experience, as devices brought along are mainly for directions or help. It's good to talk with your fellow adventurers. This book is all about that—sharing stories about outdoor life, knowledge, and experiences.

You'll find this is an interactive book that can serve as prompts for discussion or be used as a game. These are questions that people ask around a campfire, on a backpacking trip, or during some other outdoor recreational activity. There are many kinds of questions included about outdoor skills, outdoor and nature knowledge, desires to do outdoor activities, and personal experiences in the outdoors.

1

What is the most beautiful thing you have seen on the trail?

2

What was the scariest outdoor encounter you had with an animal?

3

Tell a story about paddling on a lake.

4

Do you know anyone personally who has done or attempted a thru-hike?

5

Tell a swimming or fishing story.

6

Have you gone canyoning?

7

What is an outdoor activity you would enjoy doing?

8

When was the first time you slept outdoors?

9

Have you spent a night alone in the woods?

11

How do you select equipment? Who do you rely on for advice?

10

Have you ever taken a ride in a hot air balloon?

12

Could you hunt
or fish to kill
your own food?

13

Tell a
tree house
story.

14

Do you use
hand or
foot warmers?

15

When an
adventure is done,
what do you
generally feel?

16

How often do you go to the beach?

17

Would you rather own a cabin in the mountains or a home on the beach?

18

Have you ever been lost in the woods?

19

Would you camp or do another outdoor activity on a holiday?

20

Are you good
at cooking
over a fire?

21

How do you stay
warm during
winter sports?

22

Ever fish
with a spear?

23

Have you dived off a floating dock?

25

Describe a clove hitch.

24

Have you ever splinted a bone break?

27

Do you prefer jogging in the city or in nature?

26

Are you into spooky stories or sing-alongs?

28

Tell a story about an encounter with an insect outdoors.

29

Tell a winter climbing story.

30

Do you know how to be avalanche aware?

31

Ever hear a coyote crying or a bear sniffing around your tent in the middle of the night?

32

What have been your horseback riding experiences?

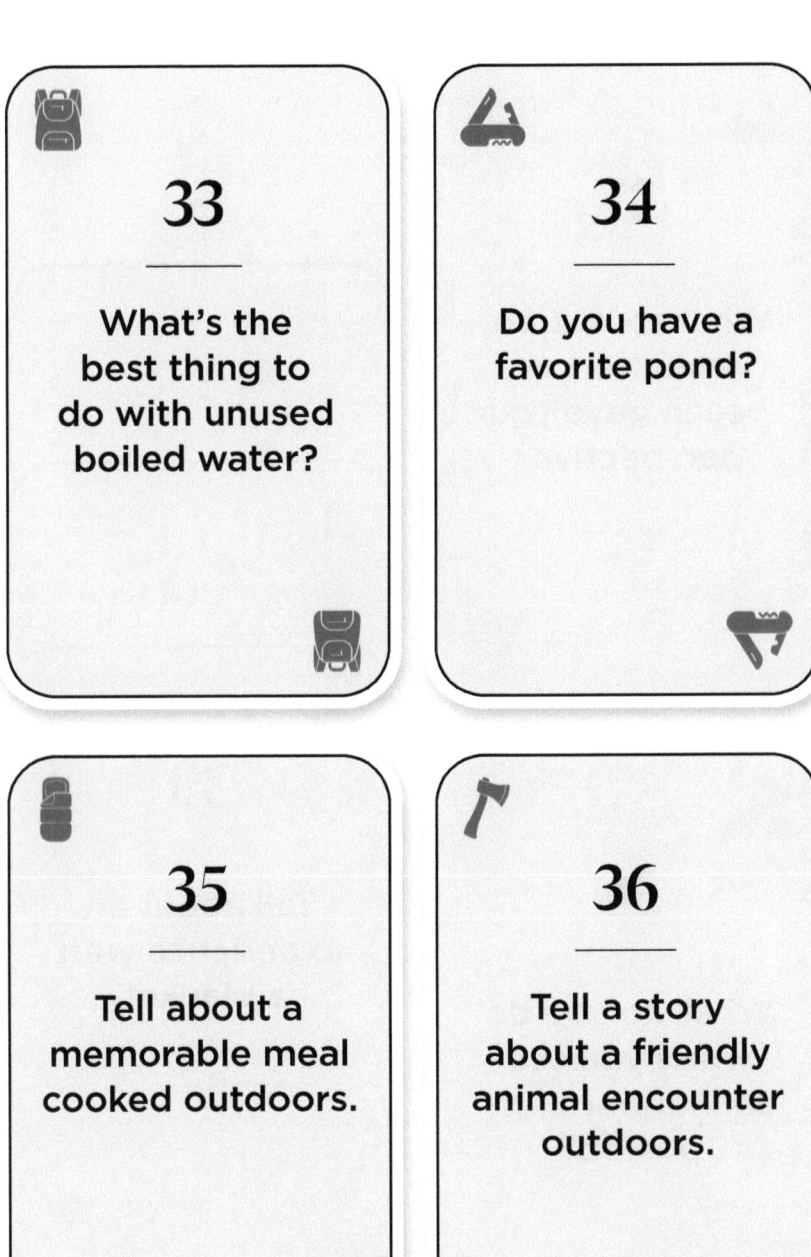

33

What's the best thing to do with unused boiled water?

34

Do you have a favorite pond?

35

Tell about a memorable meal cooked outdoors.

36

Tell a story about a friendly animal encounter outdoors.

37

What rock, tree, mountain, or ocean gave you perspective?

39

Tell about an experience with a blanket.

38

What do you do when you see animal warnings posted?

40

Can you
navigate using
your hair?

41

Share a memory
you have from
sitting around
a campfire or
stargazing.

42

Have you
ever caught
a firefly?

43

Have you camped in the snow?

44

Have you ever made a rock collection?

45

Tell about an experience learning to ride a bicycle.

46

What is your favorite bird?

47

Would you rather run a marathon or swim 5 miles?

48

Do you know how to treat a snakebite?

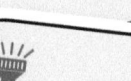

49

What's your favorite outdoor activity to do during each season?

50

Name five health benefits of outdoor activities.

51

When hiking, what is your mind usually doing?

52

Tell an igloo story.

53

What is your favorite outdoor animal to observe?

54

What wildlife have you seen in parks or gardens?

55

Have you been on a trip where there was a base camp?

56

Do you have dreams when you sleep outdoors? Are they different?

57

What is the name of the tent that goes up in a few seconds?

58

What's the most adventurous outdoor activity you've ever done?

59

Ever clean a fish?

60

Sit-on-top or sit-inside kayak?

61

Have you ever tried cross-country skiing?

62

Do you lock things up during outdoor adventures?

63

Describe a letter you wrote from camp.

64

How careful are you about your environmental impact?

65

What do you do when you see animal scat (animal poop)?

66

Do you set goals, like logging X number of miles on a bike or hike?

68

Tell about a surprise on a kayak or canoe trip.

67

Do you like a certain type of water bottle?

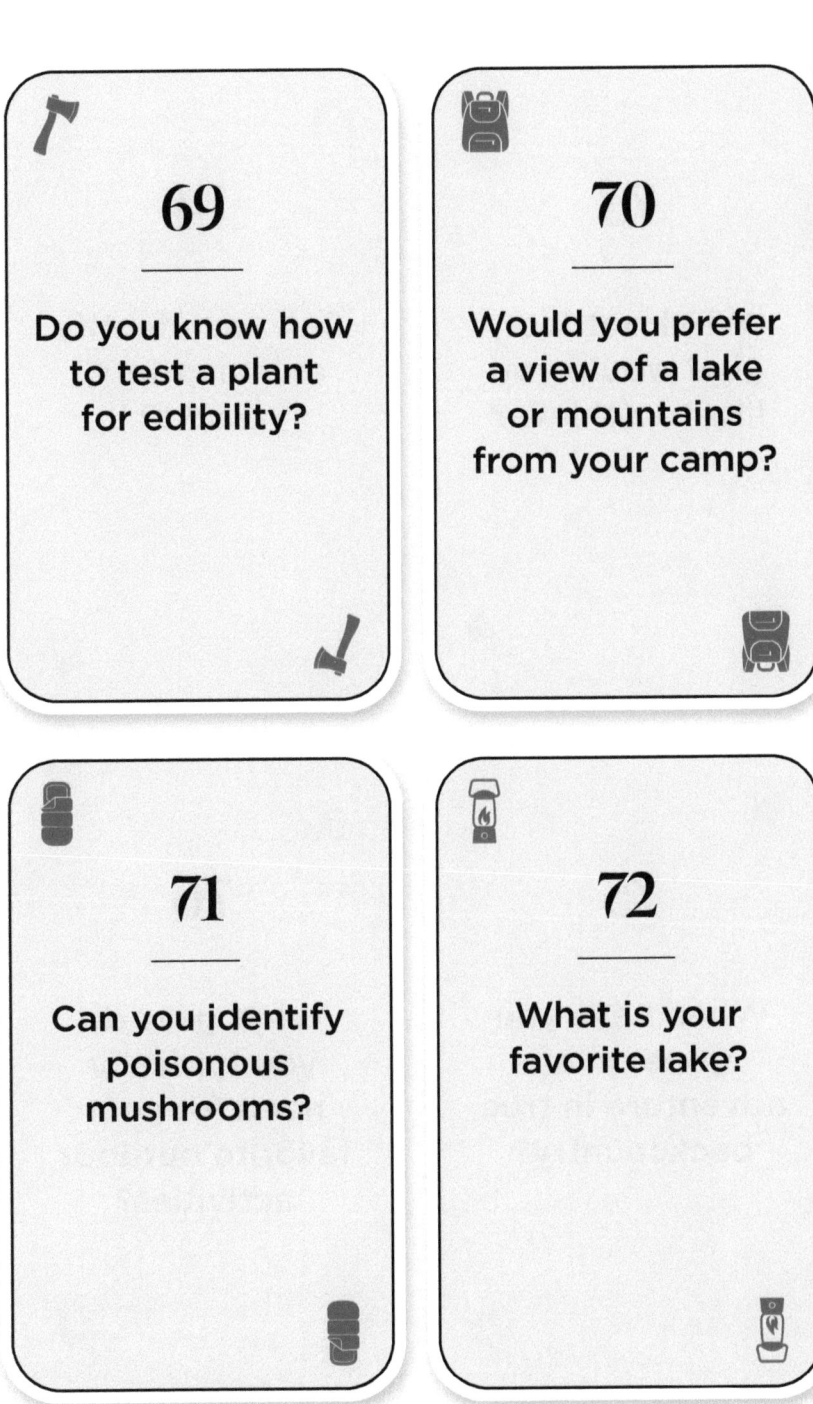

69

Do you know how to test a plant for edibility?

70

Would you prefer a view of a lake or mountains from your camp?

71

Can you identify poisonous mushrooms?

72

What is your favorite lake?

73

What outdoor goal would you like to achieve?

74

Can you identify animal prints/ tracks?

75

When have you gone on an adventure in true backcountry?

76

What gear do you typically need for your favorite outdoor activities?

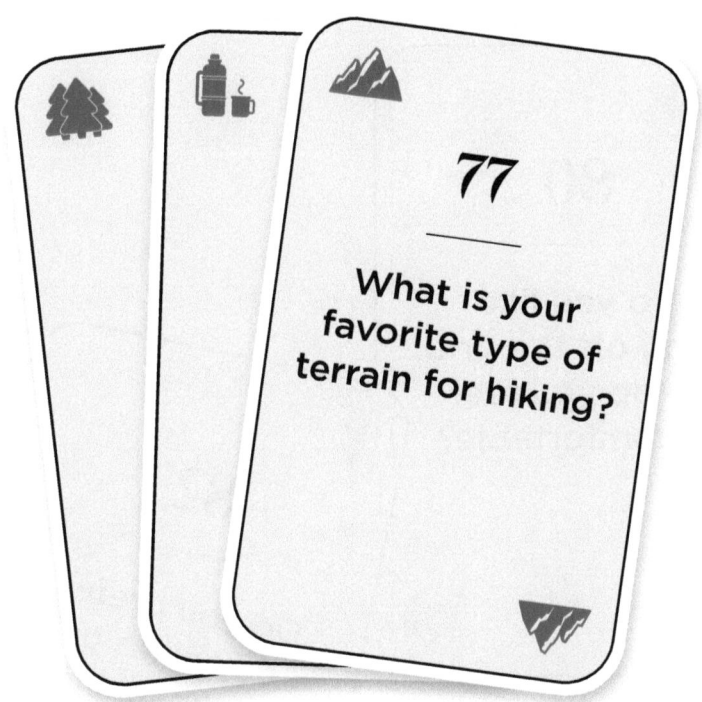

77

What is your favorite type of terrain for hiking?

78

Who do you do the most outdoor activities with?

79

How do you feel after outdoor activities?

80

Do you like being off the grid, or do you feel uncomfortable?

82

Do you prefer day hikes or backpacking overnight?

81

Can you tell about a pop-up tent experience?

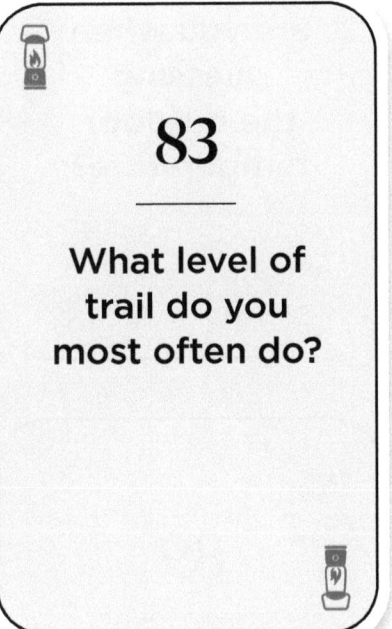

83

———

What level of
trail do you
most often do?

84

———

Describe an
adventure that
was above your
skill level.

85

———

Have you ever
run a marathon or
half-marathon?

86

Have you been on a hike or adventure with an expert guide?

87

How accurate are you when guessing the outdoor temperature?

88

Have you sketched or painted on a camping trip?

89

Lemonade or tomato juice?

90

How do you stay
safe at the beach?

91

Can you read
a compass?

92

Tell an outdoor
yoga or tai
chi story.

93

What national
parks have you
experienced?

94

What was the craziest thing you ever did in the woods?

95

Do you bike at night?

96

What do you know about natural signposts involving trees and plants?

97

If a trail becomes unexpectedly difficult, what do you do?

99

Do you recognize any of the plants around you as items you may use to season food while you're cooking outdoors?

98

Tell about something you stepped on during a hike.

100

Have you seen an owl at night?

101

Do you enjoy fishing? If you do, what type?

102

What inspired you to take to the outdoors in the first place?

103

How would you mark a trail if you wanted others to be able to follow your path in the wild?

104

If you could have been part of a past expedition, which one would you have chosen?

105

Have you tried or would you try an extreme outdoor activity or sport?

106

Can you find your way by the sun or other celestial objects?

107

Tell about a time when scissors really helped.

108

What's the most number of people you've stayed with in a tent?

109

How often do you go cycling?

110

Do you prefer visiting parks during the day or evening?

111

Describe an incident when something got frozen.

112

Have you ever had a shell collection?

113

Have you ever created a snow sled for yourself?

114

Do you know how to use GPS in the outdoors?

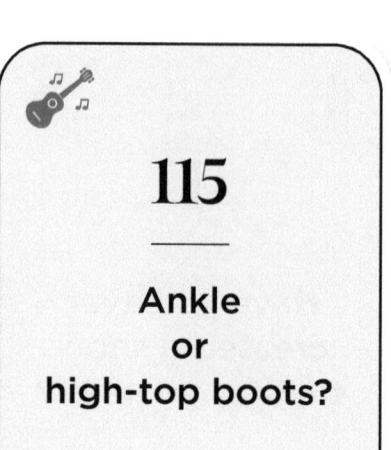

115

Ankle
or
high-top boots?

116

Do you know how
to use a CB radio?

117

Have you ever
performed CPR?

118

Tell a story about
being in a swamp
or marsh.

119

Ever soak in a natural hot spring?

120

What special feature would you like bicycles to have?

121

Would you ever do a thru-biking adventure?

122

Would you rather water-ski or snow-ski?

123

How can we be innovative for adaptive adventure?

125

Ever kayak or canoe at night?

124

Do you shower when camping? Any tips to make it not so weird?

126

How would you describe the vibes you get from being active outdoors?

127

Do you ever heed your grumpy muscles and slow down while biking?

128

Have you ever slept in a portaledge?

129

Cave or tree house?

130

What do you do if it starts raining while you're camping?

131

If you could go camping at any national park, which one would it be?

132

Do you like to catch or forage for your own food?

133

Have you ever capsized in a boat or kayak?

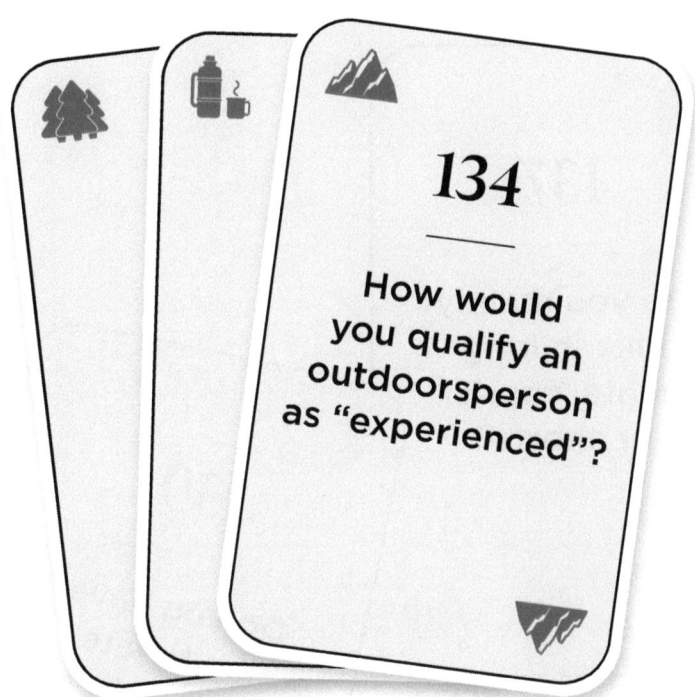

134

How would you qualify an outdoorsperson as "experienced"?

135

What item are you more likely to forget to take on a camping trip?

136

Do you have a post-hike routine?

137

Do you mainly hike in long pants, capris, or shorts?

139

Do you have legitimate climbing shoes?

138

As you hike far away from it all, what are you thinking about?

140

Do you consider yourself a naturophile?

141

What beverage refreshes you best after a hike or other outdoor activity?

142

Can you deal with being without internet and TV outdoors?

143

Describe stinging nettles.

144

Have you ever tried skiing or snowboarding?

145

Do you prefer cycling alone or in a group?

146

How do you stay safe while camping in the wild?

147

Tell about an experience walking on ice.

148

What do you know about packing/gear load distribution?

149

Tell a story about a time you roasted marshmallows at a campsite.

150

Ghost stories or funny stories?

151

When was the last time you lost track of time in the outdoors?

153

Would you walk through a forest alone at night?

152

Have you made snow angels?

154

What do you
do to recover
after strenuous
outdoor activity?

155

Tell a story about
lying in the grass
or among flowers.

156

Tell a
poncho
story.

157

Have you ever done section hiking?

158

What do you smell? Are there any distinct scents in the air? What are they, and what do they remind you of?

159

Go hiking or fishing, soak in a hot spring, or just chill at the campsite?

160

What trail apps have you tried? Which is your go-to?

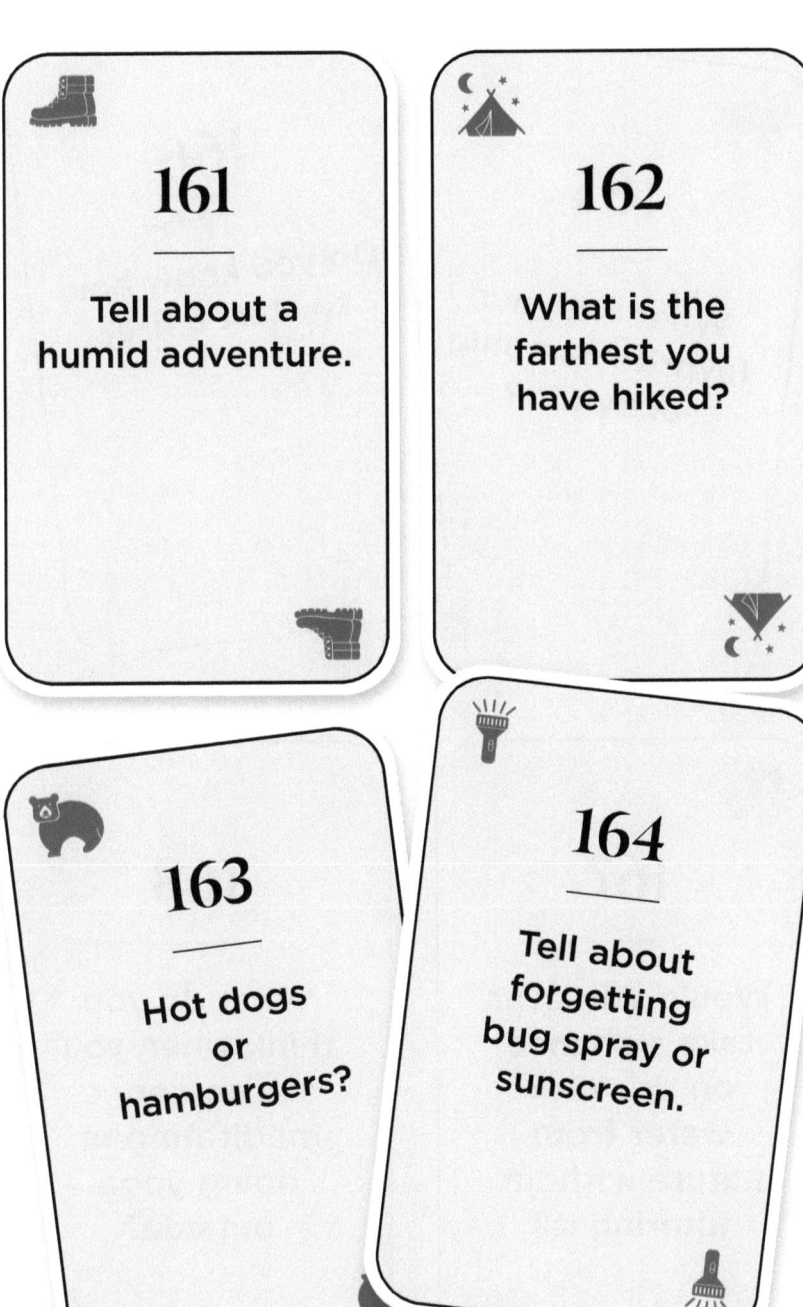

161

Tell about a
humid adventure.

162

What is the
farthest you
have hiked?

163

Hot dogs
or
hamburgers?

164

Tell about
forgetting
bug spray or
sunscreen.

165

What are your favorite camping activities?

166

Do you know how to start a fire?

167

Would you ever take a chance on drinking water from nature without filtering it?

168

What do you think when you see someone meditating or doing yoga outside?

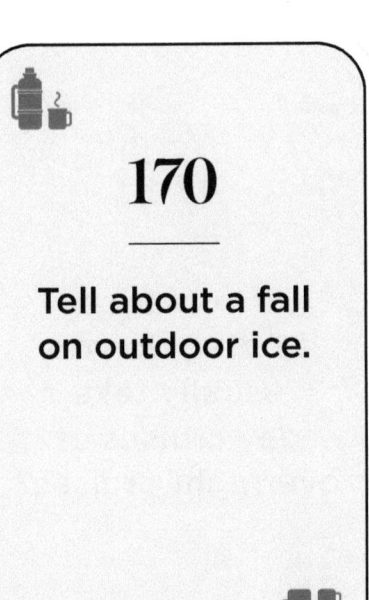

170

Tell about a fall
on outdoor ice.

169

Describe a historic
snowball fight.

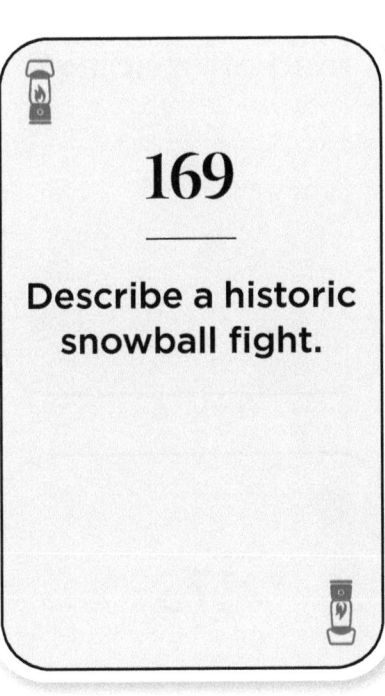

171

Do you prefer
camping when
it is busy or
not busy?

172

If you are a boater, do you usually take day cruises or overnight cruises?

173

Have you ever tried off-roading?

174

Tell about a time when you forgot your gloves.

175

Have you ever listened to a forest ranger presentation?

176

Have you ever
gone skydiving?

177

Where would
you like to go
surfing and why?

178

How do you
stay safe during
winter sports?

179

Play in snow
or
play in sand?

180

Describe an awe-inspiring experience in the outdoors.

181

Have you ever been stranded on a boat?

182

Do you know how to give various forms of first aid?

183

What's the last thing you did outside?

184

Have you been on a powerboat?

185

Could you tell the time outdoors without a watch or other device?

186

What were your favorite outdoor activities as a child?

187

Have you ever had to drag or haul heavy gear or supplies?

188

Describe an unexpected animal encounter.

189

What tastes better outside than inside?

190

Have you come across any cool outdoor videos or movies?

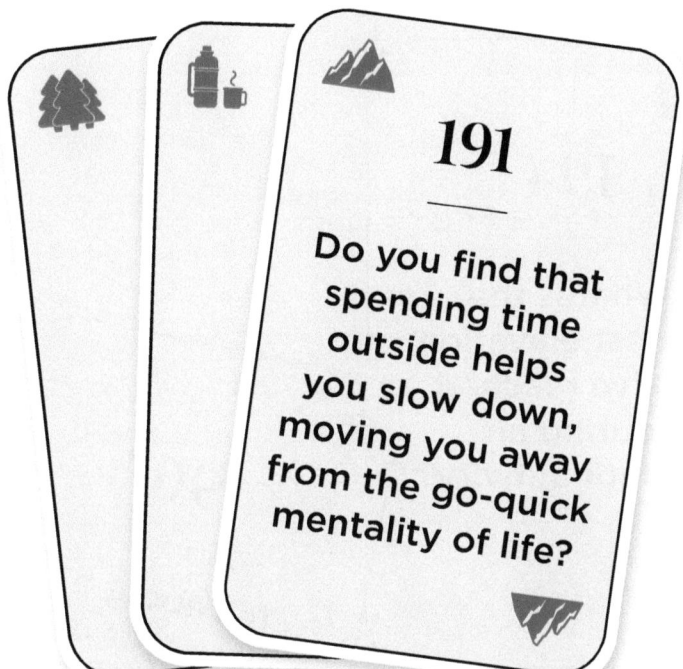

191

Do you find that spending time outside helps you slow down, moving you away from the go-quick mentality of life?

192

Would you prefer a campground with a pool or a playground?

193

Describe what is called the "joy of cycling."

194

What is the highest elevation you've reached during an outdoor activity?

196

Tell about a wet socks or shoes experience.

195

If you could camp anywhere in the world next weekend, where would you go?

197

Do you regularly update your outdoor checklists?

198

What do you think about fastpacking, distance trail running and ultralight backpacking combined?

199

What is a reef knot?

200

What was your favorite campsite based on the scenery?

201

How often do you go swimming?

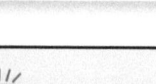

202

Ever see someone arrested during a camping trip?

203

What do you think about hikers competing for fastest known times (FKTs)?

204

Have you swum in
tropical waters?

205

What is the worst
thing you can
imagine having
to eat to survive
in the wild?

206

Have you ever
been in a boat
during a storm?

207

When did you
learn to swim
and how?

208

Would you go on a yearlong (or close to yearlong) outdoor trip?

210

On what type of bike are you most comfortable?

209

Are you loyal to certain outdoor brands?

211

Describe a
favorite childhood
memory in nature.

212

What do you
think animals
are saying to
one another?

213

Have you ever
gone bird-
watching?

214

Would you like to do a bike tour, staying at a different motel every night?

215

Tell a story about a time you were outdoors during a lightning strike.

216

What do you like to do in a swimming pool?

217

Have you ever built a snowman or had a snowball fight?

218

Tell a story of a time you got lost outdoors.

219

Have you tried windsurfing?

220

Describe a very long night you had in the outdoors.

221

Describe a time you were stranded during an outdoor experience.

222

Have you ever attempted a triathlon?

223

How do you feel about hot-weather hiking?

224

When was a time you did not wear the right clothes outdoors?

225

Do you have a favorite camping spot for weekend getaways?

227

Have you done an adventurous outdoor activity solo?

226

Who was the most interesting person you met in the outdoors?

228

Do you have a waterproof breathable raincoat?

229

Tell about
an alligator
experience.

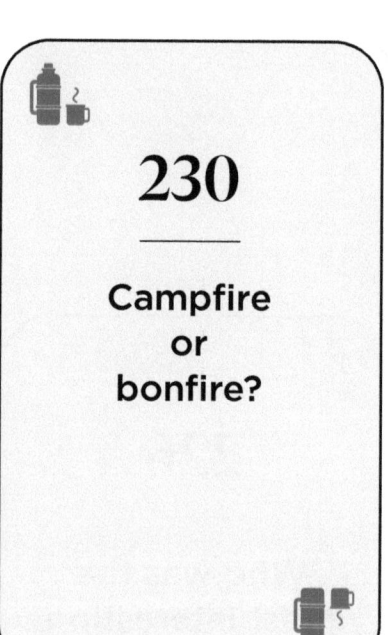

230

Campfire
or
bonfire?

231

How long could
you sit on a rock?

232

What are some
good high-calorie
snacks you
recommend for
the outdoors?

233

Do you know how to improvise a signal mirror?

234

What's your favorite camp dessert?

235

Hiking
or
mountain biking?

236

Have you ever visited a national park in the winter?

237

What natural phenomenon or act of nature would you like to see if you would be safe?

239

Describe the sound of your bike bell or horn.

238

What plants can you identify?

240

What does HYOH stand for and mean?

241

What is a fisherman's knot?

242

Do you prefer the ocean or the forest?

243

Explain declination.

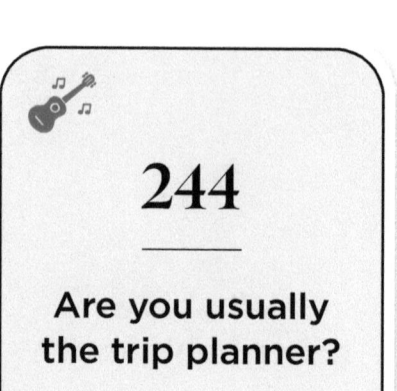

244

Are you usually the trip planner?

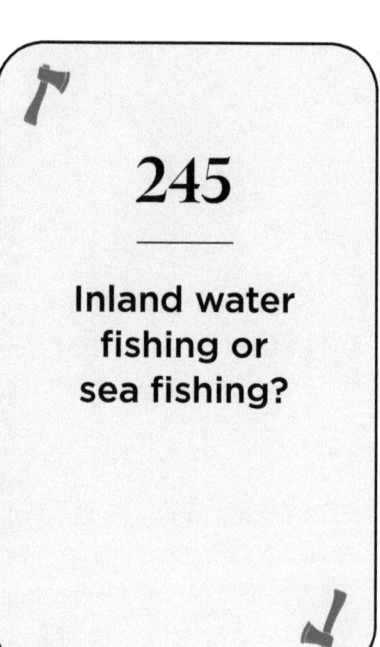

245

Inland water fishing or sea fishing?

246

Who is your favorite outdoor adventurer or one you admire the most?

247

Tell about walking with a blister.

248

Mountains you want to climb, literally.

249

Tell about an outdoor scavenger hunt.

250

What are the best tips and tricks to starting a campfire? Should we bring firewood with us?

251

What experience
made you feel
close to nature?

252

Picnic
or
barbecue?

253

How and when
did you get your
first bike?

254

Tell an inflatable mattress story.

255

When camping and looking for a spot, what three things should you look out for?

256

What is your favorite loop trail?

257

How would you treat a jellyfish sting?

258

Headlamp or flashlight?

259

What is in your ditty bag?

260

How have you learned outdoor skills?

261

What was the
most memorable
walk you've
ever taken?

262

Do you prefer
a night or
morning walk
in the woods?

263

Have you seen a
whale or a pod
of whales?

264

Do you buy
special insoles for
shoes and boots?

265

Describe where you went on your last walk and what you saw.

266

Have you ever worn gaiters?

267

Describe a bivvy you used and why.

268

Describe an unexpected visitor or encounter with another person in the outdoors.

269

How do you stay motivated to exercise outdoors?

270

Take a few minutes to close your eyes and listen to the trail around you. What are some of the noises you hear? Where are they coming from?

271

What place would you think of as a hiker's paradise?

272

What is your favorite activity to do on a boat?

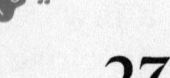

273

Tell a story about your favorite outdoor scent.

274

Tell about a calm after a storm.

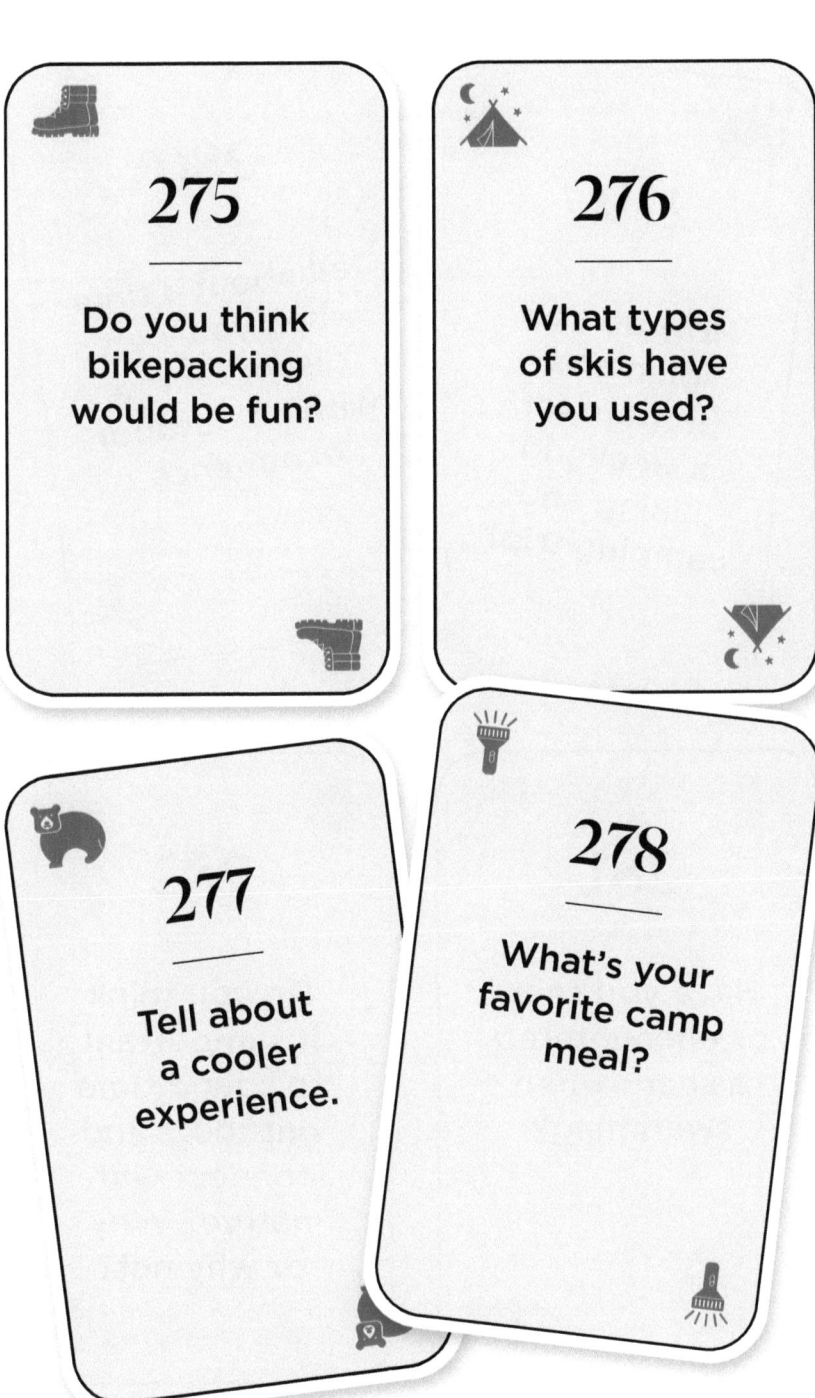

275

Do you think
bikepacking
would be fun?

276

What types
of skis have
you used?

277

Tell about
a cooler
experience.

278

What's your
favorite camp
meal?

279

How do you plan and prepare for a weekend hiking and camping trip?

280

Tell about a time when you were disappointed with an outdoor experience.

281

Have you seen or encountered a shark when swimming?

282

Do you think it's important to spend time outdoors and connect with nature? Why or why not?

283

Do you use or avoid DEET products?

284

Would you ever go on a last-minute camping trip?

285

Ever used crampons?

286

Tell about the craziest or scariest camping experience you've had.

287

What is one thing you would not do to survive in an emergency situation?

288

Would you wear a fanny pack?

289

What is cowboy camping?

290

If you could make any dessert over the campfire tonight, what would it be?

291

Do you use social media when hiking or camping?

292

Tell a story about teaching someone how to ride a bike.

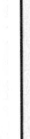

293

How often do you take part in outdoor activities?

294

Tell a story about a downed tree on the trail.

295

What is a hot spot, and do you know what to do for one?

296

What is the farthest you have biked?

297

How often do
you exercise
outdoors?

298

Tell a story about
the moon.

299

What are some of
the challenges you
face while hiking
or camping?

300

Do you enjoy
action/adventure
vacations or
relaxing ones?

301

Tell a
waterfall
story.

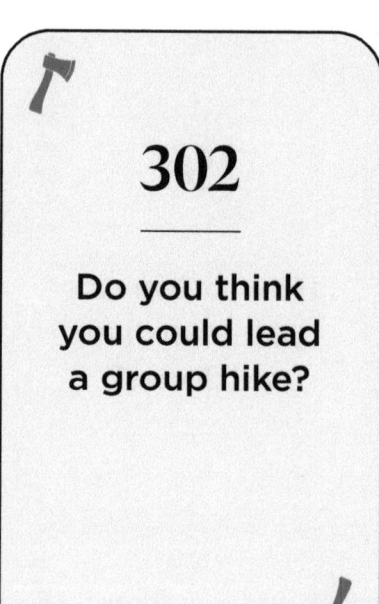

302

Do you think
you could lead
a group hike?

303

Do you think of
trail running as an
extreme activity?

304

Have you ridden
a horse or biked
in the woods?

305

Do you read about the history of the places where you do outdoor activities?

306

When was the last time you visited a national park?

307

Would you like to have an adventure cat or dog?

308

Can you make a
figure-eight knot?

310

Are you skilled
with a knife?

309

Tell about an
experience of
discouragement
or disappointment
in the outdoors.

311

Why do you participate in outdoor activities?

312

Do you prefer a sleeping bag or a cot with a blanket?

313

What water sports do you enjoy?

314

Have you
ever gone
snowboarding?

315

When was the last
time you watched
the sun rise?

316

Do you often go
for walks? If you
have a walking for
exercise routine,
what is it?

317

Tell a story about
a memorable
walk on a beach.

318

Would you rather be given gear you want or an outdoor experience as a gift?

319

Would you rather walk 1 mile or run ten 100-yard sprints?

320

Do you believe in Bigfoot or other legendary creatures?

321

Describe an alien experience.

322

Tell about getting down from a cliff.

324

Describe a time when fog was a big part of a recreational situation.

323

What are the outdoor recreation opportunities in the town you live in now?

325

Would you
know what to
do if someone
suffered an
allergic reaction?

326

Tell about a
memorable
camping
experience.

327

Ever sleep
outdoors?

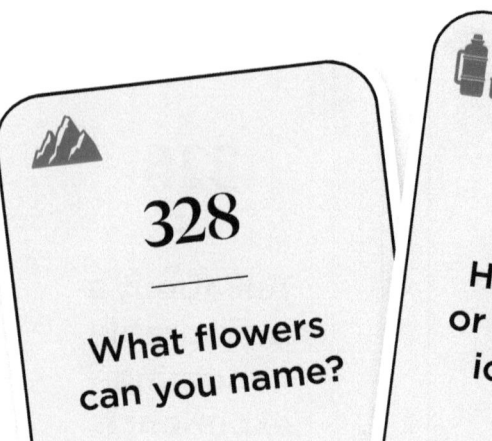

328

___

What flowers can you name?

329

___

Have you done or would you try ice climbing?

330

___

What colors do you most love to see in nature?

331

___

Have you ever had a wild animal break into your tent?

332

Tell a story about improvised music during an outdoor activity.

333

If you caught a fish, would you eat it or throw it back?

334

Tell what campfire food you find easy or hard to cook or eat.

335

Tell about an experience of joy in the outdoors.

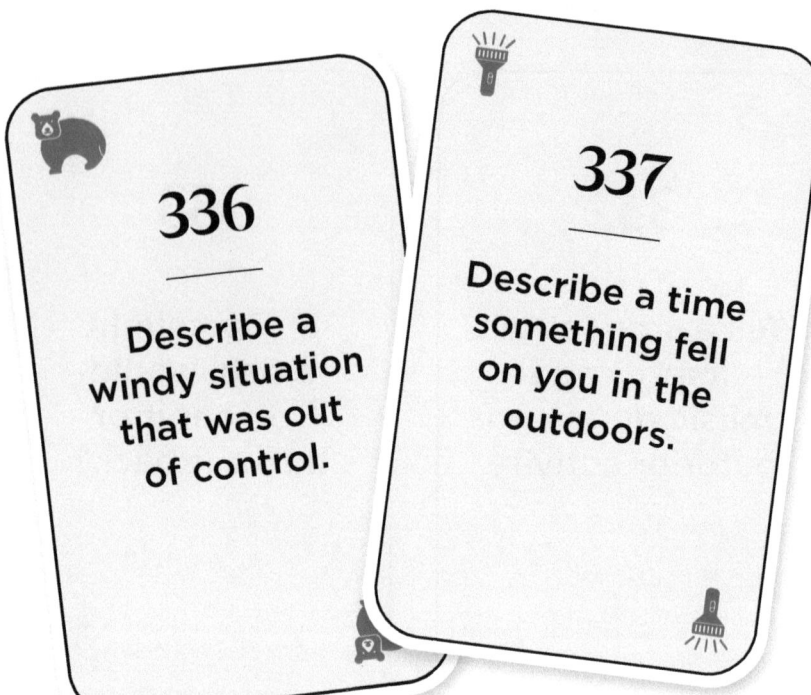

336

Describe a windy situation that was out of control.

337

Describe a time something fell on you in the outdoors.

338

Have you ever had to open a bottle or can without an opener?

339

Tell a story about something that got tangled.

340

Do you prefer
to camp with
friends or family?

341

Tell about
camping with
a best friend.

342

What is the worst
part of camping?

343

Describe a difficult zipper experience.

344

What is Naismith's rule?

345

Would you like to attend a National Outdoor Leadership School?

346

Discuss a super-interesting documentary or docuseries about the outdoors.

347

Tell about a favorite or surprising sign you saw in a park.

348

Tell about sleeping on the ground.

349

Have you ever built a lean-to?

350

What are the best times and days for you to be more active?

351

What is your interest in underwater activities?

353

Tell how outdoor adventure builds your resilience.

352

If you could have any comfort from home on your camping trip, what would you bring with you?

354

Could you navigate with the help of a watch?

355

When was the last time you went for a long walk?

356

Tell a tale about reaching a fork in a trail.

357

Do you go on a First Day hike each year?

358

Tell about a
time when a saw
came in handy.

359

Tell a
headlamp
story.

360

How do you
organize your
outdoor gear?

361

Tell about a time
you fell into water.

362

What is your favorite park or garden to visit?

363

Have you been in a yurt?

364

Tell a summer camp story or two.

365

Did you go to
summer camp
when you
were a kid?

367

Do you seek out
places to hike,
ride, or camp that
have historical
significance?

366

Tell what you
know about
fish bait.

368

Tell about an
unlikely friendship
you formed in
the outdoors.

369

Are you more
comfortable in
warm weather or
cool weather?

370

What would you
do if there was
wildfire smoke
in your area?

371

Did you ever pack food that spoiled and got you or others sick?

372

Guitar or harmonica?

373

Have you ever participated in an outdoor fitness class?

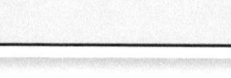

374

What is the longest (timewise) cycling trip you've taken?

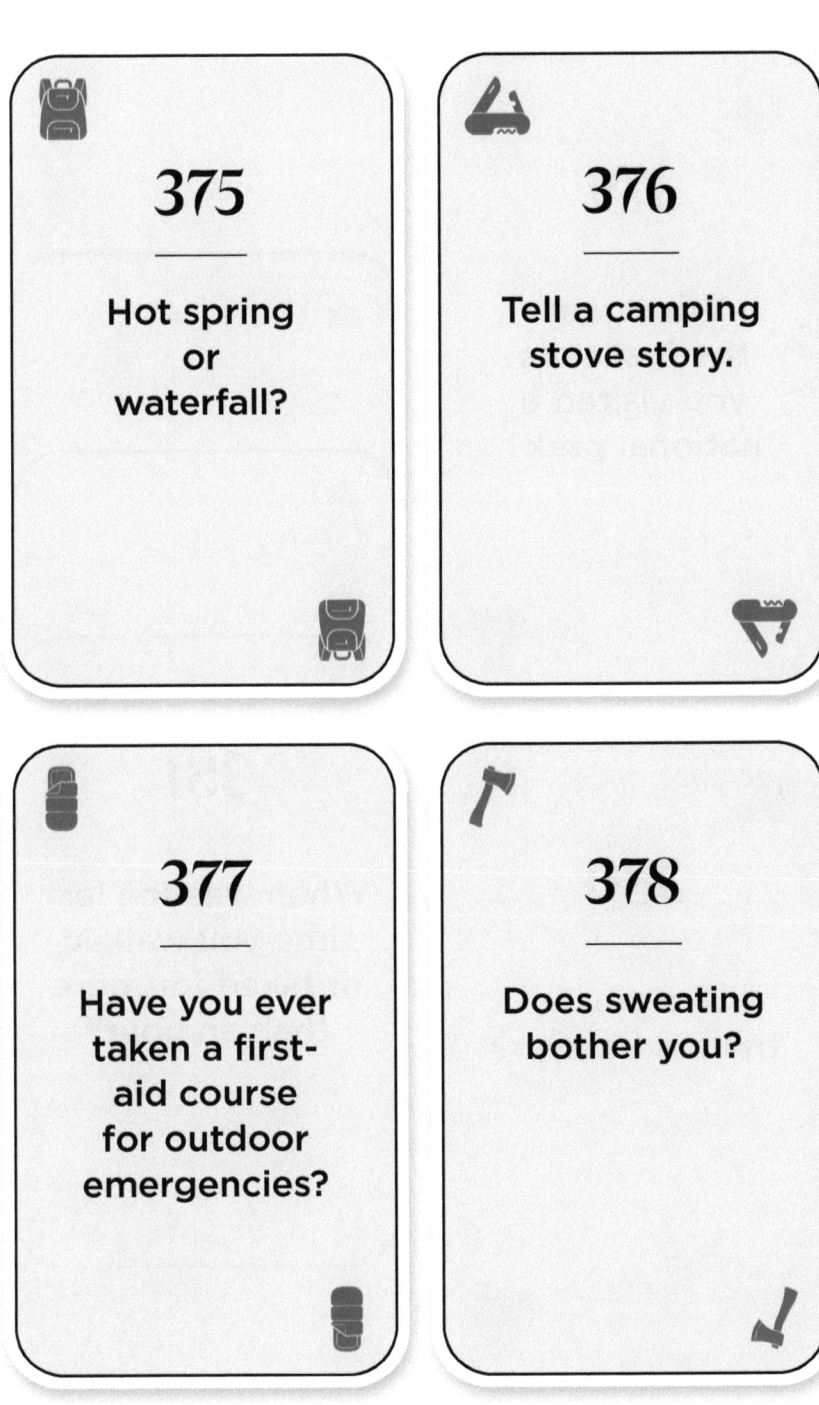

375

Hot spring
or
waterfall?

376

Tell a camping
stove story.

377

Have you ever
taken a first-
aid course
for outdoor
emergencies?

378

Does sweating
bother you?

379

When was
the first time
you visited a
national park?

380

Are you a
trained belayer?

381

When was the last
time you walked
or hiked for more
than an hour?

382

Can you make a granny knot?

383

Describe a time you got caught in a storm when hiking or exercising outdoors.

384

What is your favorite hiking trail?

385

Tell about losing something in the outdoors that you really needed.

386

Tell about the last time you felt joy outside.

387

Tell a shoelaces story.

388

If you had no toilet paper, would you use a leaf or . . . ?

389

Have you done
a zip-line or
rope course?

390

What are the
best snacks you
have had during
an outdoor
excursion?

391

Have you ridden
in a glider?

392

Tell about
a sledding
experience.

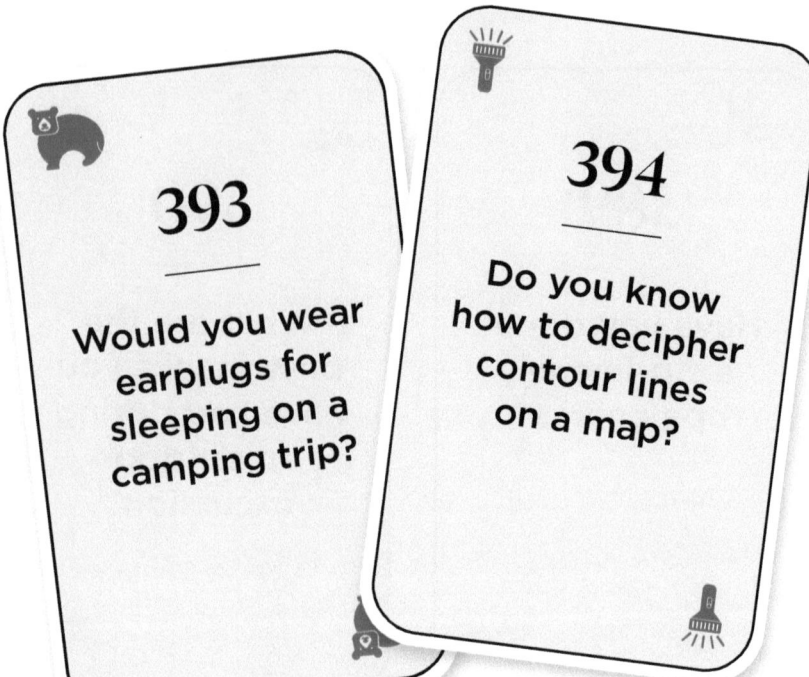

393

Would you wear earplugs for sleeping on a camping trip?

394

Do you know how to decipher contour lines on a map?

395

Tell how you avoid injury and also know when not to do something risky.

396

Tell a backpacking story.

398

What is the
most rugged
activity you have
participated in?

397

What course or
courses would
you like to take to
learn or improve
outdoor skills?

399

Do you prefer
the sound of
crickets or frogs?

400

Have you ever done a Christmas run or Christmas bird count?

401

Do you have any tips for someone new to hiking?

402

Do you prefer to adventure close to home, or are you a road tripper?

403

What outdoor activities haven't you tried yet?

404

What are all
the places you
have camped?

405

Do you take
breaks, or are you
usually powering
through a hike?

406

Tell about a chair
or tent collapse
or a leaky tent.

407

Do you favor
relaxed or
tight clothing
for outdoor
activities?

408

What do you think is the whole point of camping?

410

What camps have you attended?

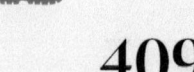

409

What type of outdoor exercise do you enjoy?

411

What are your favorite camp shoes?

412

What birdcalls do you know?

413

Tell a rainy trip story that ended up being great.

414

Which type of tree bark is best for lighting a campfire (birch, oak, ash, hazel)?

415

Describe a moment of trail magic.

416

What trees can you name?

417

Do you care what your hair looks like when doing outdoor activities?

418

Tell about an experience with mud.

419

Do you carry a tool kit for whatever your outdoor activity is?

420

Do you know how to patch a bike tube? Change or repair a bike chain?

421

What is the most challenging hike you've done?

422

What do you like
to tell stories
about in the
outdoors?

424

Have you ever
used emergency
signaling?

423

Roadkill:
Eat or
drive away?

425

———

What bicycle
accidents have
you had?

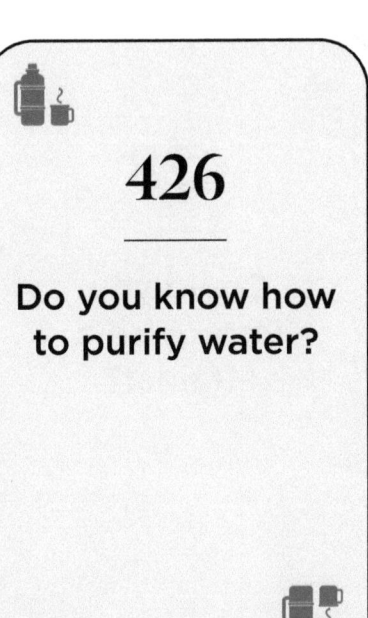

426

———

Do you know how
to purify water?

427

———

Have you crossed
a rope bridge?

428

Could you improvise a strainer?

429

What is the tent called where the poles crisscross and intersect to form triangles?

430

Have you ever discovered a hidden waterfall?

431

Have you ever been part of a sponsored expedition?

432

Tell about something you found in your backpack or gear that was unexpected or scary.

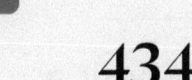

433

Have you swum in a clear mountain lake?

434

What animal would you consider to be your spirit animal and why?

435

Tell a rope story.

436

How many miles
a day could you
hike consistently?

437

Have you camped
in the backyard?

438

Tell about a
childhood
experience with
swimming.

439

Compared to others, do you spend more or less time in the sun?

440

What were the outdoor recreation opportunities in the town you grew up in?

441

Have you ever had to bushwhack through backcountry without trails?

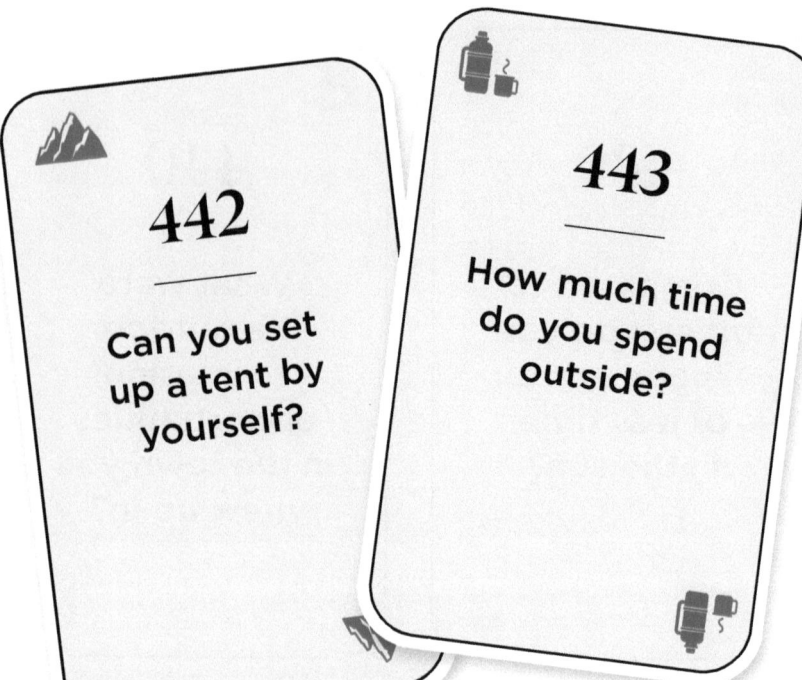

442

Can you set up a tent by yourself?

443

How much time do you spend outside?

444

Name everything you'd need to bring if you wanted to cook beans on toast.

445

Do you prefer to camp for a few days, a week, or a month?

446

Tell about a time playing hide-and-seek or tag.

447

What is your favorite river?

448

If you could live in a cabin in the woods, would you?

449

What food on a stick have you eaten outdoors?

450

Have you camped in a desert?

451

Tell what you think is the most awesome outdoor feat.

452

Describe an inspiring nature walk you have taken.

453

What outdoor survival skills do you want and need to learn?

454

Have you ever done sea fishing?

455

Do you have a favorite piece of camp swag or camping gear (clothes, water bottle, stickers, etc.)?

456

If you are/ were an expert paddler, would you consider thru-paddling a major river?

457

Have you ever done archaeology in your backyard?

458

Tell about a trip with no cell phone signal.

459

What is your favorite beach?

460

Have you ever had a gourmet meal on a camp stove?

461

What is the most beautiful animal?

462

Tell about something or someone who got stuck.

463

Ever belong to a hiking club?

464

Can you recognize any types of animal scat?

465

Do you practice introspection when spending time alone outdoors?

467

Have you ever been camping in a foreign country?

466

How would you treat a beesting?

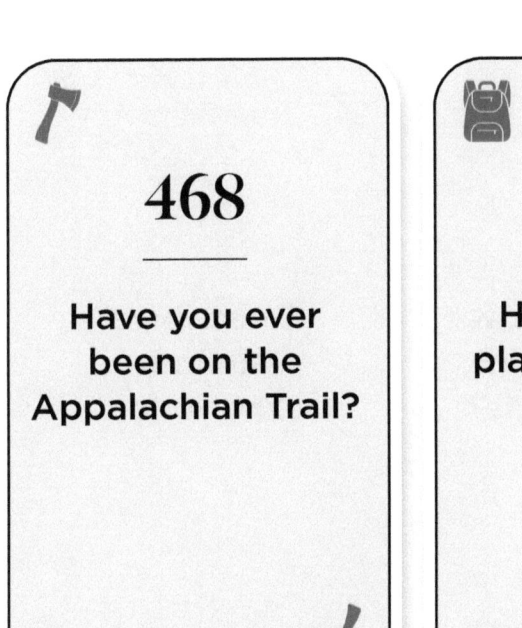

468

Have you ever been on the Appalachian Trail?

469

Have you ever played disc golf?

470

Tell about a time paddling a canoe or kayak.

471

If you are a runner, have you tried trail running?

472

Do you know how
to walk a straight
line in the woods?

473

Describe a
summit
experience.

474

Have you ever
seen an avalanche
in the wild?

475

Do you have
hiking or
biking goals?

477

Ever ride a
water bike?

476

Which of these
navigation
techniques are
you familiar
with: aiming
off, contouring,
detouring,
handrailing,
standoff/attack
point, zigzag
routes?

478

What are some
outdoor activities
you like to do in
your local area?

479

What knots do
you know how
to make?

480

What is the best
climbing outfit?

481

Do you ever
temper the pace
of your run to
make it easier
to talk with your
running buddies?

482

What is the most beautiful object in nature?

483

Have you ever been car camping?

484

Car camping or backpacking?

485

Is there anything more useful than aluminum foil when it comes to cooking when camping?

486

Have you eaten campfire-cooked pizza?

487

Describe what you know about choosing outdoor footwear and socks.

488

Tell a story about a tick encounter.

489

How do you feel about e-bikes?

490

Have you ever reeled in a big fish?

491

Can you identify different types of ticks?

492

Do you prefer fall, winter, spring, or summer camping?

493

What should you do if you need to poo in the wilderness?

495

Tell about bandaging a wound.

494

Where would you like to in-line skate and why?

496

Tell a story
about a personal
flotation device.

497

Have you ever
taken an outdoor
photography
class?

498

What have
you used to
filter water?

499

Tell a story about a bag that broke.

500

Do you usually try spur trails?

501

How would you signal for help?

502

What activities do you like to do in a park?

503

Can you take a bearing?

504

Would you want to picnic in a meadow or forest?

505

Tell a sandals story.

506

Describe an unforgettable sunrise or sunset.

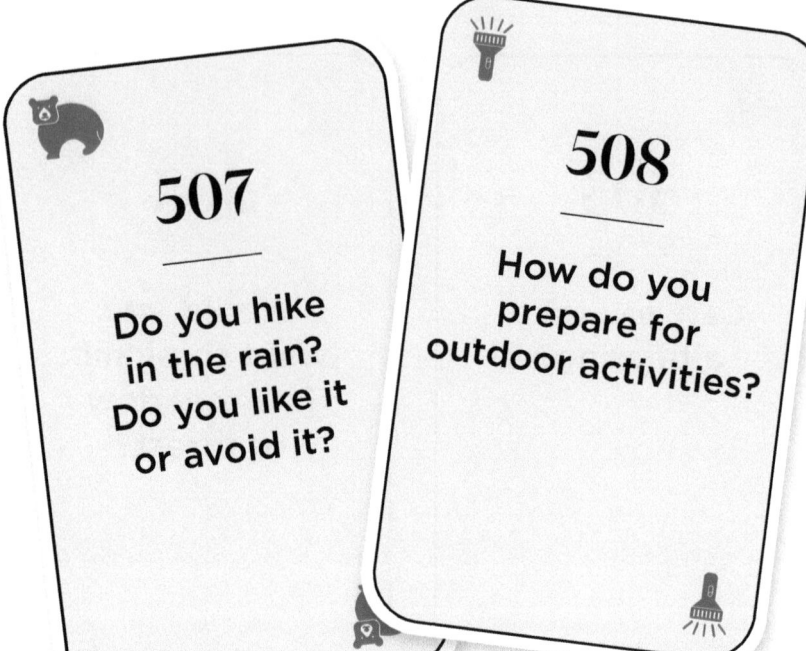

507

Do you hike
in the rain?
Do you like it
or avoid it?

508

How do you
prepare for
outdoor activities?

509

Have you ever
helped blaze
a trail?

510

Have you ever
gone snorkeling
or scuba diving?

511

Have you used
a flare gun
or flares?

512

What do you
appreciate most
about being in the
great outdoors?

513

Describe
something you
had to sew or
a wardrobe
malfunction.

514

Tell a caterpillar story.

515

Do you agree with or resent the term "micro trail" in reference to a hiking trail of 2 miles or less?

516

Ever been ice fishing?

517

Have you done off-trail/unmarked navigation?

518

Do you know how to perform CPR?

519

Would you rather skydive or hang glide?

520

Do you know the meaning of trail blazes and markers?

521

What is one irrational or unusual item you would want to bring if you climbed a really high mountain?

522

What have you used as a fire starter?

523

Tell a story about flashlight tag.

524

Do you prefer hiking hills or walking level ground?

525

What's the highest level of trail you've done?

526

Tell a port-a-potty story.

527

Have you used old-fashioned snowshoes?

528

Do you prefer hiking alone or with others?

529

Tell what you think a dingle stick is.

530

What's your favorite outdoor activity to do on the weekend?

531

Nature: What do you stand most in awe of?

532

What activities do you wear a helmet for?

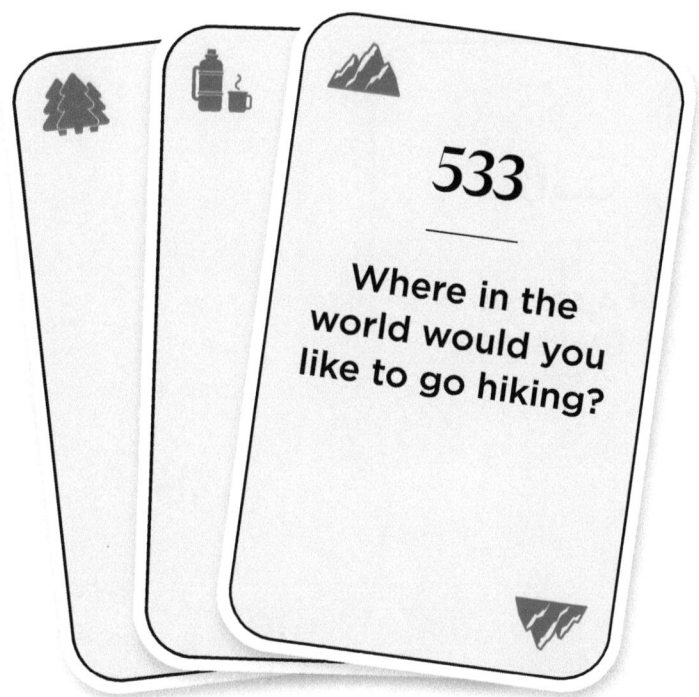

533

Where in the world would you like to go hiking?

534

How do you check the weather before an outdoor activity?

535

Have you ever felt the need to mark your trail so you can get back safely?

536

Tell a ran-out-of-fuel story.

538

Have you ever hiked a glacier?

537

Can you name the Ten Essentials for outdoor activities?

540

What exercises do you do that complement or enhance your outdoor activities?

539

Tell about having no access to showers or bathing facilities.

541

Have you ever built a cairn?

542

Who was/is your favorite camping partner?

543

How long do you need to boil water to kill any parasites in it?

544

Have you seen a shooting star?

545

Campfire
or
camp stove?

546

Do you feel more connected or disconnected in the outdoors?

547

Describe your most dangerous prank at camp.

548

Do you prefer sleeping in a tent or a cabin?

549

Discuss the topic of access for wheelchair-bound and other disabled people who want to enjoy the outdoors.

550

Tell about a time when you were pleasantly surprised about an outdoor experience.

552

What is the best color for a tent?

551

Do you do anything special to care for your feet or hands?

553

—

Tell about a shadow puppet experience.

554

—

Would you prefer no bugs or no rain in the outdoors?

555

—

Tell a snowshoeing story.

556

Is there an object you found and kept from a hike?

557

Describe improvised toilet paper you have used.

558

Tell about a surprise when swimming.

559

Have you seen a meteor shower?

560

Do you ever eat gorp, and what is your combination of things?

561

What is the most important safety tip for outdoor adventures?

562

Ever meet up with a bear on a hike?

563

Have you ever rescued a person or an animal in the outdoors?

564

What is the highest you climbed on a mountain?

565

Do you ever listen to outdoor podcasts?

566

Do you have a go-to campsite?

567

Are you competitive with others or yourself, even in outdoor activities that are not competitions?

568

Would you like to own a kayak, canoe, or other boat?

569

Do you have a packing list of essentials to bring for your outdoor activities?

570

Have you been on a nature treasure hunt?

571

What thoughts and feelings come to mind when you think of play?

572

Do you have a "season" for your hiking and other outdoor adventures?

573

Do you wear goggles for swimming?

574

Have you ever hiked above the tree line?

575

Do you wear reflective clothing and have reflectors on your gear?

576

Have you ever eaten in complete darkness outside?

577

Have you seen a coral reef up close?

578

What was the first time you had an inspiring outdoor experience?

579

Have you ever improvised a spoon?

580

**Sing-along
or
storytelling?**

581

What survival skills do you have and are confident in?

582

What campfire games have you played?

583

Would you rather live on an island or a mountaintop?

584

What type of hat do you prefer in winter, rain, sun?

585

Do you have an outdoor tradition on a holiday like Thanksgiving or First Day?

586

What kind of
pillow do you use
for camping?

587

What was the
best and what was
the worst place
you camped?

588

Ever tried
Nordic walking?

589

As a child, did
you have a special
place in nature?

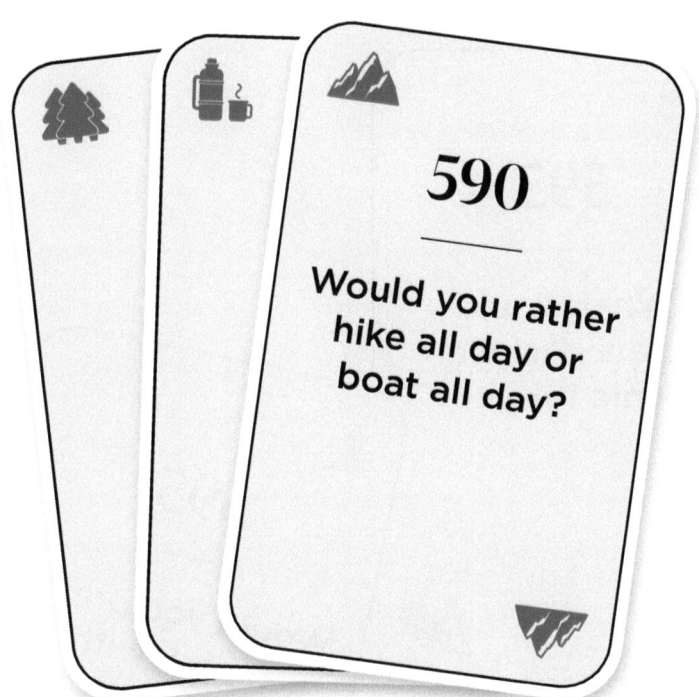

590

Would you rather hike all day or boat all day?

591

Have you ever built a raft?

592

Have you ever sketched flowers or leaves you see on the trail, or perhaps a landscape you find particularly breathtaking?

593

What would
be a perfect
picnic for you?

595

Would you prefer
a park with
wildlife or rock
formations?

594

Have you ever
been sponsored
in a race?

596

Do you prefer a long hike without hills or changes in elevation or a challenging change of elevation?

597

What is your favorite outdoor sport to watch?

598

Describe a time when you felt at peace in the outdoors.

599

Describe
a ghost
experience.

600

Can you
fix a flat
bike tire?

601

Do you know
how to clean
a hydration
bladder?

602

Would you be
able to rescue
someone with
your swimming
skills?

603

Do you document
your hikes and
other outdoor
activities?

604

Do you have a
favorite outdoor
adventure book?

605

Do you know how
to split firewood?

606

Do you enjoy
camping?

607

Have you ever gone on a safari or wildlife tour?

608

What is the most difficult terrain for you to hike through?

609

Have you ever built a survival shelter?

610

What is your favorite outdoor term/word?

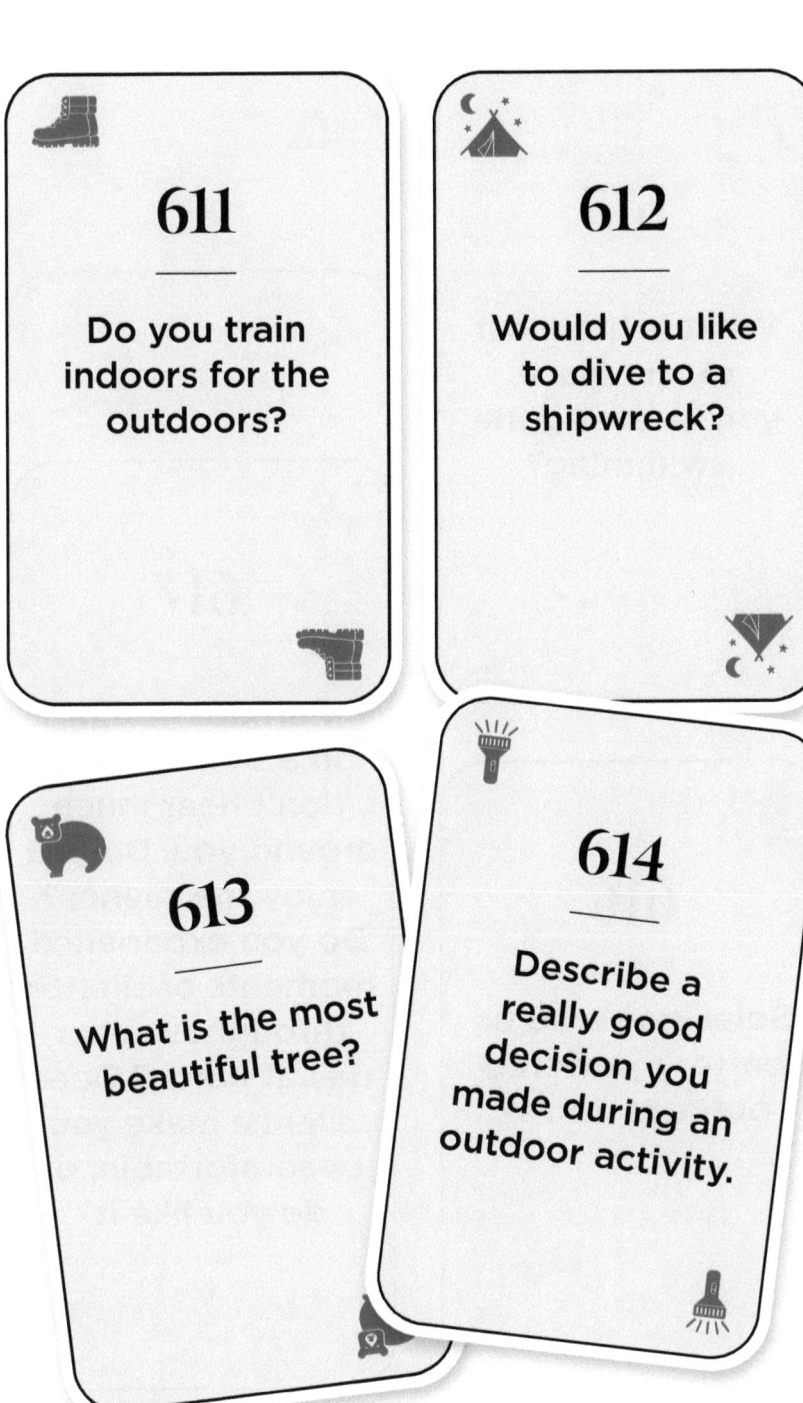

611

Do you train indoors for the outdoors?

612

Would you like to dive to a shipwreck?

613

What is the most beautiful tree?

614

Describe a really good decision you made during an outdoor activity.

615

What is the most exotic place you've ever gone swimming?

617

Perhaps you're on a trail and you don't hear much around you. Do you enjoy the silence? Do you experience moments of silence throughout your day at home? Does silence make you uncomfortable, or do you like it?

616

Solar-powered or battery-powered outdoor items?

619

———

Do you know how
to navigate using
pace counting?

618

———

What is your best
memory from a
camping trip?

620

———

Have you tried
rock climbing
or bouldering?

621

Did you grow
up camping?

622

Have you ever
paddled to
an island?

623

Contact lenses
or glasses
for outdoor
activities?

624

What's your
favorite memory
involving nature?
What makes
the memory
so special?

625

What is your best energy-getting snack?

626

Do you sleep on a cot, a mattress pad, or an air mattress; or do you sleep on the ground?

627

Will you adventure outdoors when you get old?

628

Tell a story about a time you meditated outdoors.

629

Have you ever been bitten by a spider while outside?

630

What do you learn from outdoor activities?

631

Do you clean your water bottle regularly?

632

What is your opinion on wearing a bike helmet?

633

Who was your worst travel companion in the outdoors?

634

What is your preferred number and type of pockets on a coat?

635

Do you know how to cauterize a wound or otherwise stop bleeding?

636

What was the stupidest thing you have worn outside?

637

Do you know the names of clouds, or are you familiar with what their shapes indicate?

638

Describe an outdoor experience when you felt like an outsider.

639

Have you ever bought used outdoor gear or borrowed gear to try it out?

640

What creatures have you brought home from a camping trip, dead or alive?

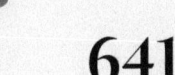

641

Should snowboarding be allowed on ski slopes?

642

How do you stay safe while cycling?

643

Have you worn night-vision goggles?

644

Solo or tandem kayak? Paddle or pedal?

645

Do you like hearing only the sound of the wind on a hike?

646

What is one outdoor trip you would like to go on in this lifetime?

647

Do you like to walk barefoot outdoors?

648

Describe an overpacking experience.

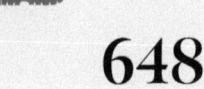

649

Do you enjoy hiking?

650

What is the
most amazing
natural wonder
you've seen?

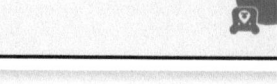

652

Tell a
mesh screen
story.

651

Do you leave your
itinerary with
someone before
an adventure?

653

Have you
stayed in a
camper van?

654

What item are
you most likely
to forget to take
on a hike?

655

Tell a fun fact
you know
about a plant.

656

What is your favorite outdoor activity?

657

Tell a story about trying to blow up something with air, like an air mattress.

658

Have you ever found treasure outside?

659

Think of your favorite smell. Is it something that could be found in nature? If not, what's its closest nature equivalent?

660

Ever use a
pee bottle
or pee cloth?

661

Tell about an
experience
walking in
deep snow.

662

Tell a
skunk
story.

663

What is
your go-to
camping tool?

664

Describe something that happened while paddling on a body of water.

666

Have you tried snowshoes?

665

Do you like to read guidebooks?

667

What tree did
you like to climb
as a kid?

668

Have you ever
gone skiing?

669

Do you usually
play sports
outdoors?

670

Ever improvise a plate?

671

How would you improvise a cup?

672

How do you care for your outdoor-activity shoes?

673

Have you taken a pet on an outdoor adventure or camping?

674

Tell a story about ignoring a weather forecast.

675

Ever have to improvise an oar or paddle?

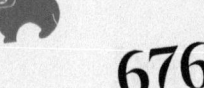

676

Do you use and recommend trekking poles?

677

Describe your first time in a canoe or kayak.

678

Tell a camera story.

679

Do you dream of thru-hiking? Would you ever attempt it? If yes, under what circumstances?

680

When was the last time you walked a distance in the rain, caught by surprise or done on purpose?

681

What are the tents that hang on a mountain called?

683

Tell about a
memorable
bicycle riding
experience or
incident.

682

Describe a
time you left
something behind
in the outdoors.

684

What food do
you prefer to eat
when camping or
backpacking?

685

Are you a good swimmer, or do you need more instruction/ confidence?

686

Tell a story about setting up camp.

687

Do you exercise outside when you are sick?

688

What kind of hiking and camping experiences do you like to have on the weekends?

689

What is
the most
beautiful flower?

690

Tell a
sunburn
story.

691

When buying a
sleeping bag,
what does the
TOG rating mean?

692

What would you
like to see in the
wilderness more
than anything?

693

Ever wear pogies
(hand covers for
cold weather)?

694

Name uses for
nylon cord.

695

What is the
windiest situation
you have been in
when doing an
outdoor activity?

696

Steak or chicken cooked outdoors?

697

Tell about an encounter with hunters.

698

Do you wear braces or compression items for any activities?

699

What is the best bike safety tip you would share?

700

Do you have
more shoes for
outdoor activities
or regular life?

701

Popcorn
or
s'mores?

702

What is the most
number of hours
or miles you
biked in a day?

703

Do you prefer
playing games or
doing something
creative after
finishing a hike?

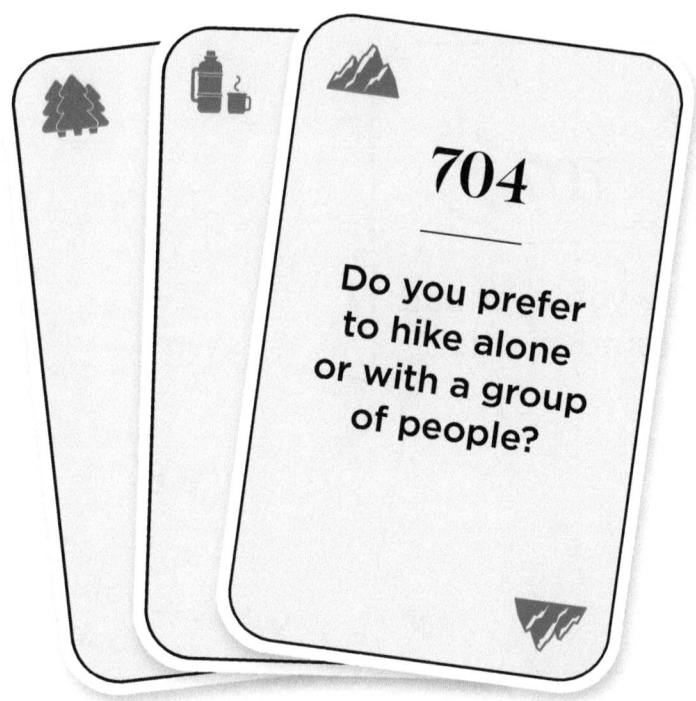

704

Do you prefer to hike alone or with a group of people?

705

Can you read a topographic map?

706

Have you ever caught a fish bare-handed?

707

Have you ever had
to remove a tick?

709

What is your
favorite sound
in nature?

708

What does it
mean to be
outdoorsy?

710

Do you spend less time with technology when you are outdoors?

711

What forest would you like to see?

712

Describe a hut you stayed in or visited.

713

What animals
really scare you?

714

What is
a fall line?
A tree line?

715

Describe an
animal you first
saw in the woods.

716

Tell about a
touch football
experience.

717

What is the coolest or most unusual rock you've found?

718

Have you ever done seaside camping?

719

Tell a story about a fake snake, spider, or other prank/ practical joke done in camp.

720

Describe a grill experience.

721

Camp on the beach or in the mountains?

723

Tell about an experience with bears at your campsite.

722

Have you ever camped somewhere without a permit?

724

Would you rather
sleep in an RV
or a tent?

725

Do you use
sweatbands?

726

What do you
like to talk about
when outdoors?

727

___

Do you know
how to tape
a sprain?

728

___

How do you
stay fit in your
"offseason"?

729

___

Have you gone
glamping?

730

___

Do you like
sleeping outside
in cold weather?

731

Do you enjoy urban hiking?

732

Have you ever had an encounter while running or jogging?

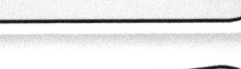

733

Would you prefer trail mix or s'mores for dessert?

734

Tell a story about tripping over something outdoors.

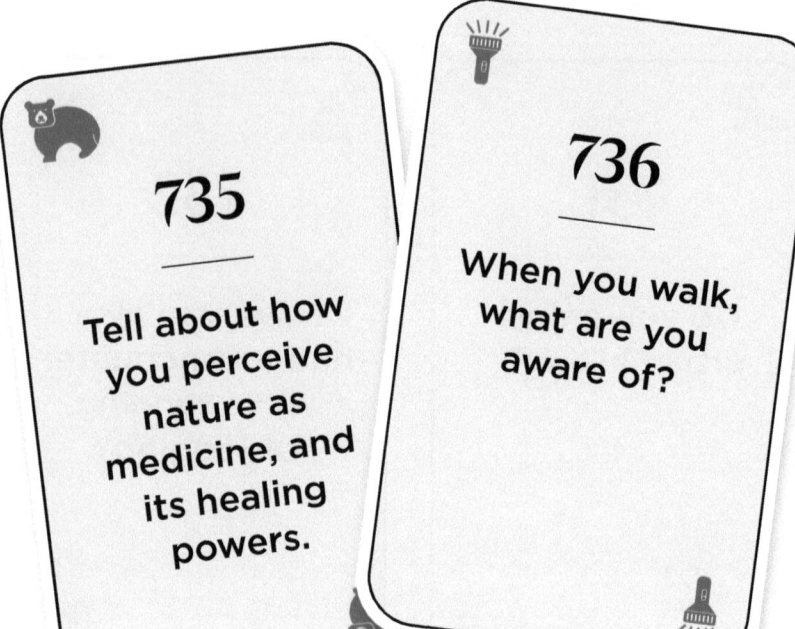

735

Tell about how you perceive nature as medicine, and its healing powers.

736

When you walk, what are you aware of?

737

What friendly animal did you expect to be unfriendly?

738

Have you ever explored a cave?

739

Ever see a fight during a camping trip?

740

Do you recount your camping adventures to others who do not camp?

741

How do you feel about people who have children attempting dangerous outdoor feats?

742

What is your
favorite winter
outdoor activity?

743

Do you like
sleeping out in
hot weather?

744

Can you make an
overhand knot?

745

Have you
ever used
an ax?

746

Could you
navigate using
the sun?

747

Can you identify
safe mushrooms?

748

What was your
most memorable
time on water?

749

How do you put
out a campfire
properly?

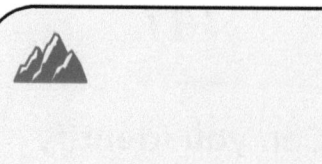

751

Do you know how to take a heading?

750

Is there a particular landscape element that you look for on a hike, like a waterfall or a certain type of tree? Why do you look for it? Did you find one of those things on your hike today?

752

Have you swung off a rope into a lake?

753

What is your
favorite type
of scenery?

754

Do you have to
talk yourself into
doing outdoor
activities if
the weather is
not optimal?

755

How do you
stay safe during
water sports?

756

How seriously
do you take
fitness tracking?

757

Tell a fun fact you know about an animal.

758

What is the one animal you do not want to come across in the wild?

759

Describe what "perfect" kit or kits you have assembled (backpacking, camping, cooking, hiking, etc.).

760

Have you ever drunk glacier-fed mountain water?

761

Have you ever gotten lost while hiking?

762

How many pairs of gloves do you think you have?

763

Would you like a view of the sunrise or sunset from your tent?

764

Tell a
raft
story.

766

Have you gone
river rafting
or tubing?

765

Have you ever
had to ration
food or water?

767

Ever use a
bike trailer?

768

Have you ever
gone ultralight
camping?

769

Have you ever
slept the night
in a hammock?

770

Do you have a favorite outdoor adventure movie?

771

Tell a story about stepping in scat.

772

What food do you usually cook while camping?

773

What archaeological ruins have you come upon outdoors?

774

Have you ever
been involved
in volunteer
archaeology?

775

Have you ever
tried canoeing
or kayaking?

776

Flashlight
or
lantern?

777

Describe a
time when you
were wet and
cold outside.

778

Have you gone for a midnight swim?

780

Where is the best place you have viewed stars?

779

What is your favorite out-and-back trail?

781

Do you have a
perfect backpack
for the outdoors?

782

Are you afraid
of heights? At
what height do
you begin to feel
uncomfortable?

783

Do you know
what DWR means
for clothing?

784

What was the
stupidest mistake
you ever made
on a hike?

785

Have you
ever eaten
a flower?

786

Tell a story about
a loud growl
you heard.

787

What is an outdoor
activity bucket
list item you have
accomplished?

788

Tell about an enlightenment or realization experience in the outdoors.

789

Tell about a time you were terrified in nature or concerning nature.

790

Ever gone on a multiday canoeing or kayaking trip?

791

How do you make the most of your time while hiking and camping on the weekends?

792

What do you like to do when you visit a beach?

793

Do you tend to overplan, under-plan, or plan just right for outdoor adventures?

794

Are you interested in learning how to forage for your food?

795

Have you ever camped alone?

796

Would you prefer to be a lifeguard or a camp cook?

797

Do you layer clothes and, if you do, in a particular way?

798

How deep into the woods have you gone?

799

Do you stop and
smell the flowers?

800

Tell about
something
that happened
after dark in
the outdoors.

801

Do you know how
thick ice has to
be to be safe?

802

Tell about
a bat
encounter.

803

Do you resist the urge to run back home after an outdoor activity and instead carve out time to savor nature?

804

What animal did you expect to ignore you but did not?

805

What is your favorite ski area?

806

Have you stayed in a tiny house?

807

How do you cook food when you're camping?

809

Ever stay in an abandoned building?

808

Tell about eating dehydrated food.

810

Would you like
to Nordic ski
to a remote
winter cabin?

811

Can you surf,
or would you
like to learn?

812

Have you ever
helped with trail
maintenance
or cleanup?

813

When you're
picking wood
for firewood,
where should
you get it from?

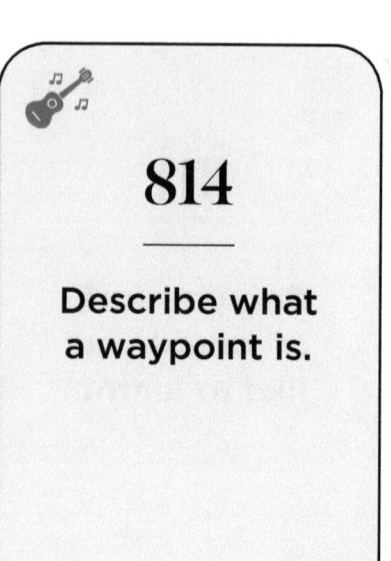

814

Describe what
a waypoint is.

815

Hiking
or
swimming?

816

Do you like
winter sports?

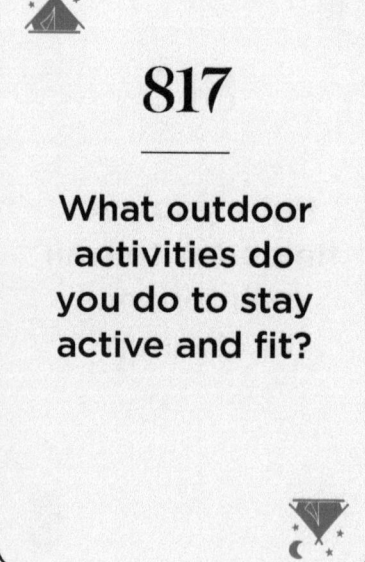

817

What outdoor
activities do
you do to stay
active and fit?

818

Tell what you know about camping/campsite etiquette.

819

Describe a strange noise you heard when outdoors.

820

Can you navigate with a map and compass?

821

Do you enjoy
picnics in parks
or gardens?

823

Describe
climbing your
first mountain.

822

What outdoor
gadget would you
love to have?

824

What parks did
you frequent
as a child?

825

Do you get into
National Trails
Day, Earth Day,
or other outdoor-
related holidays?

826

Tell about a
shoe/boot
situation.

827

What ways do you know of to collect water in the wild?

828

Do you watch videos of others' outdoor adventures?

829

Do you prefer using an outhouse or making a cat hole?

830

Tell a story about forgetting utensils, cups, or plates.

831

Would you prefer to roast marshmallows or hot dogs?

832

What is on your bucket list of outdoor activities?

833

What do you do when camping? Do you find tent time relaxing, or do you get bored?

834

Have you ever gotten seasick?

835

What is the most
beautiful garden
you've visited?

837

Tell a favorite
beach day story.

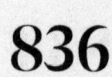

836

Do you run
or jog?

838

What is the most
expensive item
you take camping
or hiking?

839

What is your
favorite
picturesque
outdoor place?

840

Do you pack a
bungee cord?

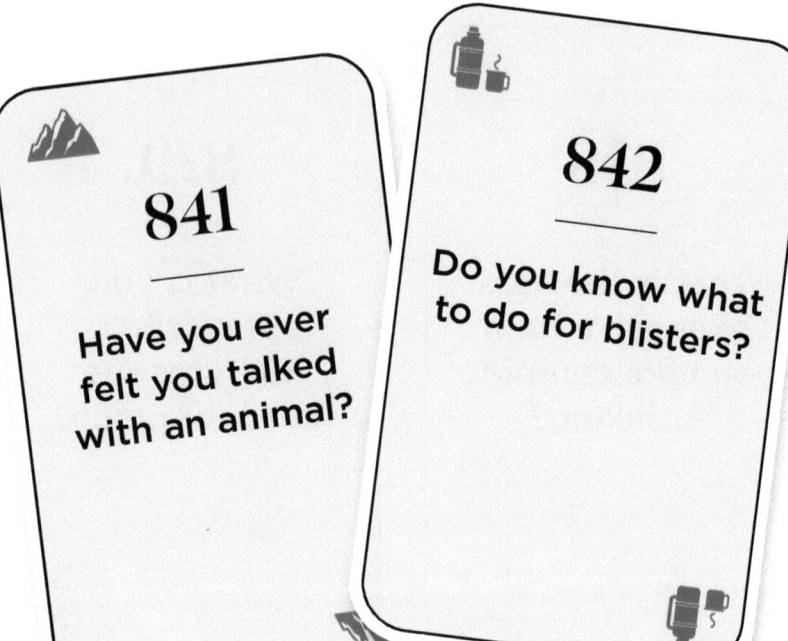

841

Have you ever felt you talked with an animal?

842

Do you know what to do for blisters?

843

What is the most number of hours or miles you hiked in a day?

844

Have you seen the Northern Lights?

845

Describe a
time when you
accidentally
left food out or
did not pack
it properly.

846

Do you have
planned outdoor
recreation?

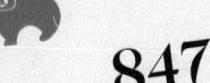

847

What is
something
in nature
you would
like to bottle
and sell?

848

How do you heat
up your tent or
keep it cool?

849

Describe a time outdoors when you pushed yourself further than you thought you could go.

850

Do you know how to treat frostbite or hypothermia?

851

Ever been rescued by a lifeguard?

852

Do you prefer a high-tech camp or minimalist?

853

Describe your
first camping trip.

854

Are you calm
or unnerved in
an emergency
situation?

855

Have you ever
gotten sunburned
in winter?

856

Fishing or bird-watching?

857

Describe what a rest step is.

858

Have you ever set up a shade shelter or dug a snow cave?

859

Invent a personal s'mores recipe or choose one ingredient to add to regular s'mores.

860

How do you give back to or take care of the planet when doing outdoor activities?

861

What is in your first-aid kit?

862

How often do you go hiking or trekking?

863

Tell a story about a bird encounter.

865

Tell about gathering firewood.

864

If you had to survive in the woods, what is one thing society deems appropriate behavior that you would immediately stop doing?

866

Clipless or clip-on bike pedals/shoes?

867

What is the longest walk you've ever taken?

868

Have you tried geocaching or orienteering?

869

What effect has nature had on your faith?

870

Would you love to own a camper van? Are you cut out for van life?

871

What outdoor activities do you like to do with friends and family?

872

What would you do if you came upon a nest of insects?

873

Frame pack choice: internal or external?

874

What do you like most about hiking?

875

Tell about a time you were really cold or really hot in the outdoors.

876

Are play and leisure different things?

877

Have you hiked switchbacks?

878

Do you know
when to wait
for rescue
and when to
hike out?

880

What is
magnetic north?

879

Do you prefer
a picnic on the
beach or in
the woods?

881

What is the best drink to have around the campfire?

882

Do you have a favorite piece of outdoor cookware?

883

Do you take extra backpack straps with you?

884

Do you enjoy cycling or mountain biking?

885

What outdoor activities have you always wanted to try but feel you cannot attempt now?

886

Tell about a camping equipment repair experience.

887

Lost with no compass, how would you find your way out of the woods?

888

What pre-prepared meals and freeze-dried foods have you eaten outdoors?

889

If you're camping in bear country, name three things you can do to be bear aware.

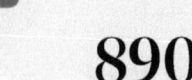

890

In camping, what is a fly?

891

What is the most interesting plant you've seen outdoors?

892

Have you used solar power in the outdoors?

893

What is your favorite tree?

894

Do you enjoy nature photography?

895

What advice would you give to someone who is new to camping?

896

Do you know how to dig a cat hole?

897

What are some must-have items for a successful weekend of hiking and camping?

898

Can you read a paper map?

899

What is the greatest name for a dog you've met in the outdoors?

900

What is something unique to you that you always have or do in the outdoors?

901

Would you like to be a scuba-certified diver?

902

Tell a rainy trip story that went south.

903

Do you find you eat more slowly in the outdoors?

904

Tell about camping on a holiday.

905

Do you wear sunglasses for outdoor activities?

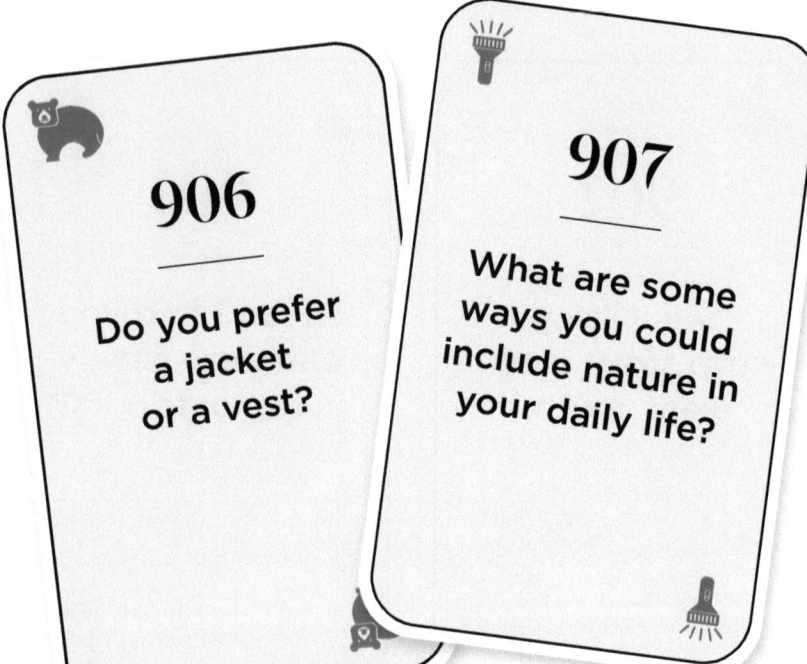

906

Do you prefer
a jacket
or a vest?

907

What are some
ways you could
include nature in
your daily life?

908

What is your
favorite memory
from a hiking trip?

909

What do you
do when you
hear animals but
cannot see them?

910

Describe a special souvenir you have from an outdoor activity.

911

Ever hire a trail outfitter to haul your gear to prearranged locations?

912

Have you ever gone mountain biking?

913

Have you ever had
or are you prone
to seasickness?

914

What is
your favorite
state park?

915

Do you prefer
a cozy cabin or
sleeping under
the stars?

916

What was your
worst night
of sleep when
camping?

917

Have you had
an outdoor job?
Would you like
one in particular?

918

What is the one
item you have
always wanted
to take with you
when camping
but never have?

919

What is an
outdoor activity
you wish you
had tried
when young?

920

Do you prefer
to camp alone
or with a group
of people?

921

What gear do you bring when you go hiking?

922

Tell about a poison ivy or other poison plant experience.

923

List your priority gear for your favorite outdoor activity.

924

Describe a search
for a lost item
outdoors.

925

Are you the
first or last to
recognize a
poisonous plant?

926

Describe
exploring a
mysterious place.

927

What lesson in
the outdoors
did you learn
the hard way?

928

Do you think
mosquito
netting works?

929

What do you
think is essential
to bring when
camping?

930

Describe a round
of charades
outside.

931

If you're camping,
how does the
campsite look
at night? How
different does the
campsite look in
the daytime?

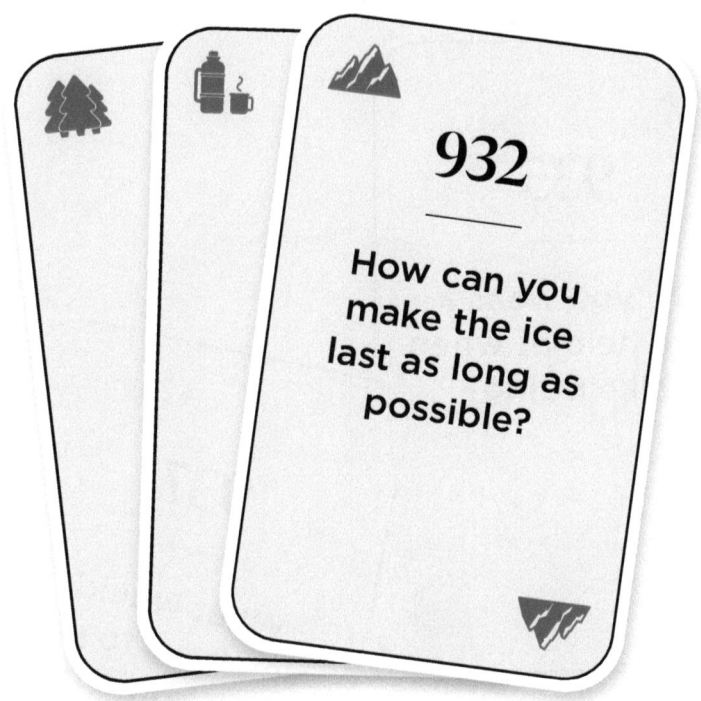

932

How can you make the ice last as long as possible?

933

Camp in an RV or tent?

934

Have you gone on a horse-drawn sleigh ride?

935

Do you wear a
bike helmet when
bike riding?

937

What would
you have to go
back home for
if you forgot
it for a hike?

936

Tell a story
about swimming
in a lake.

938

Do you like to shower at a campsite or wash up in a lake?

939

Tell a bicycle-shifting or gear-changing story.

940

What is the smallest and largest tent you've slept in?

941

What is your
favorite type of
terrain for biking?

942

Tell a camping cot
or hammock story.

943

Who was/is
your favorite
hiking partner?

944

Have you gone
fly fishing?

945

What if we took camping's goal of slowing down and applied it to our other outside pursuits?

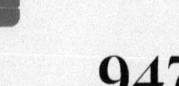

946

Describe an experience with dehydration.

947

What is a haversack?

948

Have you ever run river rapids?

949

How much water should you bring camping?

951

What is your favorite body of water?

950

Have you ever journaled in nature?

952

Have you ever
chopped wood?

953

Have you seen a
beaver dam or
other animal-built
home other than
a bird's nest?

954

Tell a
tarpaulin
story.

955

Tell what you know about hiking etiquette.

956

Have you ever found a fossil?

957

Is there a trail you have never been able to complete?

958

What would you do if you heard a coyote howl?

959

Describe Leave
No Trace
principles.

960

Do you have
a superstition
you obey in the
outdoors?

961

Would you rather
roller-skate or
ice-skate?

962

When you began
your outdoor
life activities,
what were
some beginner
mistakes
you made?

963

Do you earn your food with exercise or not connect the two?

964

Have you ever spent time on a boat (sleeping too)?

965

Tell about an experience of calm in the outdoors.

966

Have you ever had a bizarre golf experience?

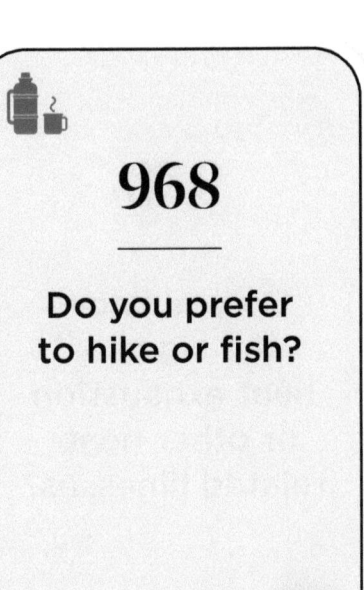

968

Do you prefer to hike or fish?

967

Have you tried gravel biking?

969

What do you think of dispersed camping—overnighting in a non-designated campground?

970

Do you know
the signs of
heat exhaustion
or other heat-
related illnesses?

971

Have you ever
portaged
a canoe?

972

Where do
you want to
camp next?

973

Tell a story
about the stars.

974

What is the
strangest thing
you have seen
on the trail?

975

Is there a brook
or creek you
would not cross?

976

Have you been
on a challenging
ski run?

977

Have you ever
considered
completing the
seven summits?

978

What do you like and not like about camping?

980

What wrong method did you use to extinguish a fire?

979

How often do you go to a park?

981

What is the largest fish you have personally seen caught?

982

Do you prefer swimming in pools or natural places like lakes and the ocean?

983

Do you carry animal repellent when biking?

984

When buying a tent, what does HH stand for?

985

What life lessons have you learned from hiking and/ or camping?

986

What was the best and the worst hike you have been on?

987

Have you crossed a river?

988

Who would you want on your Mount Everest team?

989

Do you often dress too hot or too cool for outdoor activities?

990

How are ways people can enjoy winter more?

991

What is your favorite camp song?

992

Tell a story about riding or driving a snowmobile.

994

Would you consider yourself an avid sunbather or someone who wears sunblock clothes and sunblock religiously?

993

What is your favorite outdoor sport to play?

995

Do you consider mountain climbing fun or too dangerous?

996

What is the tent called that is low to the ground, barely there, and for just one person?

997

Ever ride a bike with panniers?

998

Do you read about the geology of places where you do outdoor activities?

999

Have you been in a dense forest with hidden trails?

1001

Do you wear moisture-wicking clothing?

1000

Have you gone solo camping?

About the Author

Barbara Ann Kipfer is the author of *14,000 Things to Be Happy About* and her second-most best-selling book, *4,000 Questions for Getting to Know Anyone and Everyone*. She has written more than seventy books and calendars, including FalconGuides' *4,101 Ways Nature Makes Us Smile, Hiking Is FUNdamental, Outdoor Life Lists*, and *Hiking Ruins of Southern New England* (with Dr. Nicholas Bellantoni). Dr. Kipfer also published *1,001 Ways to Live Wild, 1,001 Ways to Be Creative, Archaeologist's Fieldwork Guide*, and *Encyclopedic Dictionary of Archaeology*.

A retired lexicographer, Dr. Kipfer holds a MPhil and PhD in linguistics, a PhD in archaeology, an MA and a PhD in Buddhist studies, and a BS in physical education. She was the first woman sportswriter for the *Chicago Tribune*. Her website is thingstobehappyabout.com.

www.ingramcontent.com/pod-product-compliance
Ingram Content Group UK Ltd.
Pitfield, Milton Keynes, MK11 3LW, UK
UKHW042104120526
5733IPUK00002B/24